SOUND INNOVATIONS

ENSEMBLE DEVELOPMENT

Chorales and Warm-up Exercises for Tone, Technique and Rhythm

INTERMEDIATE CONCERT BAND

Peter **BOONSHAFT** | Chris **BERNOTAS**

Thank you for making *Sound Innovations: Ensemble Development* a part of your concert band curriculum. With 412 exercises, including over 70 chorales by some of today's most renowned composers for concert band, it is our hope you will find this book to be a valuable resource in helping you grow in your understanding and abilities as an ensemble musician.

An assortment of exercises are grouped by key and presented in a variety of intermediate difficulty levels. Where possible, several exercises in the same category are provided to allow for variety while accomplishing the goals of that specific type of exercise. You will notice that many exercises and chorales are clearly marked with dynamics, articulations, style, and tempo for you to practice those aspects of performance. Other exercises are intentionally left for you or your teacher to determine how best to use them in reaching your performance goals.

Whether you are progressing through exercises to better your technical facility or to challenge your musicianship with beautiful chorales, we are confident you will be excited, motivated, and inspired by using *Sound Innovations: Ensemble Development*.

D1561246

ISBN-10: 0-7390-6781-8
ISBN-13: 978-0-7390-6781-9

Instrument photos courtesy of Yamaha Corporation of America Band & Orchestral Division

Concert B♭ Major

1 **PASSING THE TONIC**

2 **PASSING THE TONIC**

3 **PASSING THE TONIC**

4 **PASSING THE TONIC**

5 **PASSING THE TONIC**

6 **BREATHING AND LONG TONES**

7 **BREATHING AND LONG TONES**

8 **BREATHING AND LONG TONES**

9 **BREATHING AND LONG TONES**

CONCERT B♭ MAJOR SCALE

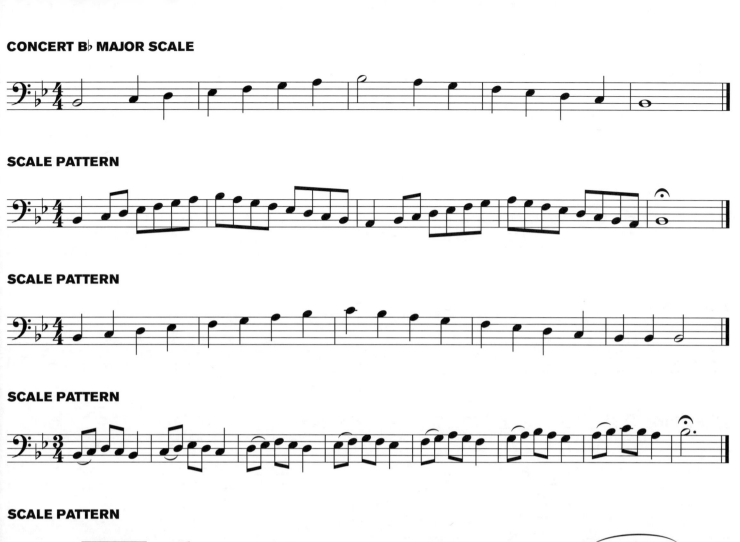

SCALE PATTERN

SCALE PATTERN

SCALE PATTERN

SCALE PATTERN

SCALE PATTERN

CHANGING SCALE RHYTHM

CONCERT B♭ CHROMATIC SCALE

18 **FLEXIBILITY**

19 **FLEXIBILITY**

20 **ARPEGGIOS**

21 **ARPEGGIOS**

22 **INTERVALS**

23 **INTERVALS**

24 **BALANCE AND INTONATION: PERFECT INTERVALS**

25 **BALANCE AND INTONATION: DIATONIC HARMONY**

26 **BALANCE AND INTONATION: FAMILY BALANCE**

BALANCE AND INTONATION: LAYERED TUNING

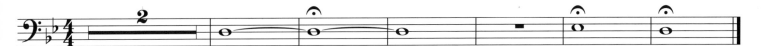

BALANCE AND INTONATION: MOVING CHORD TONES

BALANCE AND INTONATION: SHIFTING CHORD QUALITIES

EXPANDING INTERVALS: DOWNWARD IN PARALLEL OCTAVES

EXPANDING INTERVALS: DOWNWARD IN PARALLEL FIFTHS

EXPANDING INTERVALS: DOWNWARD IN TRIADS

EXPANDING INTERVALS: UPWARD IN PARALLEL OCTAVES

EXPANDING INTERVALS: UPWARD IN TRIADS

RHYTHM

36 RHYTHM

37 RHYTHM

38 RHYTHM

39 RHYTHM

40 RHYTHMIC SUBDIVISION

41 RHYTHMIC SUBDIVISION

42 RHYTHMIC SUBDIVISION

43 METER

(3+2)

8

Concert G Minor

61 **PASSING THE TONIC**

62 **BREATHING AND LONG TONES**

63 **CONCERT G NATURAL MINOR SCALE**

64 **CONCERT G HARMONIC AND MELODIC MINOR SCALES**

65 **SCALE PATTERN**

66 **CONCERT G CHROMATIC SCALE**

67 **FLEXIBILITY**

68 **FLEXIBILITY**

69 **ARPEGGIOS**

ARPEGGIOS

INTERVALS

INTERVALS

BALANCE AND INTONATION: DIATONIC HARMONY

BALANCE AND INTONATION: MOVING CHORD TONES

BALANCE AND INTONATION: LAYERED TUNING

BALANCE AND INTONATION: FAMILY BALANCE

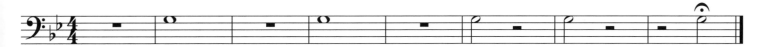

EXPANDING INTERVALS: DOWNWARD IN PARALLEL FIFTHS

EXPANDING INTERVALS: UPWARD IN PARALLEL THIRDS

79 **RHYTHM**

80 **RHYTHM**

81 **RHYTHM**

82 **RHYTHMIC SUBDIVISION**

83 **RHYTHMIC SUBDIVISION**

84 **ARTICULATION AND DYNAMICS**

85 **ETUDE**

13

CHORALE

Larghetto ... 5 ... Robert Sheldon

mf ... < f ... > mp

poco rall.

CHORALE

Moderato ... 5 ... Michael Story (ASCAP)

mf

CONCERT G MINOR SCALE & CHORALE

Chris M. Bernotas (ASCAP)

CHORALE

Moderately slow, smoothly ... 4 ... Andrew Boysen, Jr.

p

9

mf cresc. ... f

17 ... Slower

p ... rit. ... rit. ... pp

CHORALE

Sad and expressive, freely ... 6 ... 9 ... Rossano Galante

sfp ———————— f

, ... mf dim.

Concert E♭ Major

91 PASSING THE TONIC

92 PASSING THE TONIC

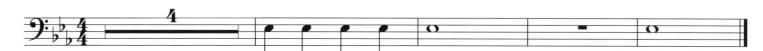

93 PASSING THE TONIC

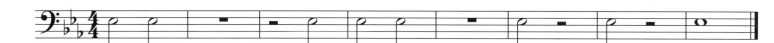

94 PASSING THE TONIC

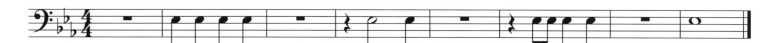

95 PASSING THE TONIC

96 BREATHING AND LONG TONES

97 BREATHING AND LONG TONES

98 BREATHING AND LONG TONES

99 BREATHING AND LONG TONES

CONCERT E♭ MAJOR SCALE

SCALE PATTERN

SCALE PATTERN

SCALE PATTERN

SCALE PATTERN

SCALE PATTERN

CHANGING SCALE RHYTHM

CONCERT E♭ CHROMATIC SCALE

108 **FLEXIBILITY**

109 **FLEXIBILITY**

110 **ARPEGGIOS**

111 **ARPEGGIOS**

112 **INTERVALS**

113 **INTERVALS**

114 **BALANCE AND INTONATION: PERFECT INTERVALS**

115 **BALANCE AND INTONATION: DIATONIC HARMONY**

116 **BALANCE AND INTONATION: FAMILY BALANCE**

BALANCE AND INTONATION: LAYERED TUNING

BALANCE AND INTONATION: LAYERED TUNING

BALANCE AND INTONATION: SHIFTING CHORD QUALITIES

EXPANDING INTERVALS: DOWNWARD IN PARALLEL OCTAVES

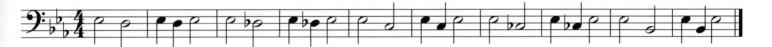

EXPANDING INTERVALS: DOWNWARD IN PARALLEL FIFTHS

EXPANDING INTERVALS: DOWNWARD IN TRIADS

EXPANDING INTERVALS: UPWARD IN PARALLEL OCTAVES

EXPANDING INTERVALS: UPWARD IN TRIADS

125 RHYTHM

126 RHYTHM

127 RHYTHM

128 RHYTHM

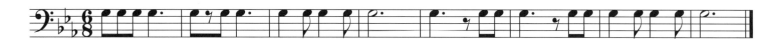

129 RHYTHM

130 RHYTHMIC SUBDIVISION

131 RHYTHMIC SUBDIVISION

132 RHYTHMIC SUBDIVISION

METER

PHRASING

PHRASING

ARTICULATION

DYNAMICS

ETUDE

ETUDE

140 **CHORALE**

Todd Stalter

Adagio, wistfully

141 **CHORALE**

Randall D. Standridge (ASCAP)

142 **CONCERT E♭ MAJOR SCALE & CHORALE**

Chris M. Bernotas (ASCAP)

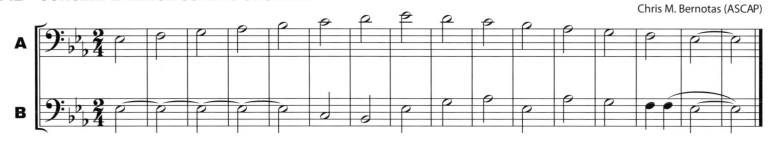

143 **CHORALE**

Michael Story (ASCAP)

Moderato

144 **CHORALE**

Andrew Boysen, Jr.

Slow and delicate

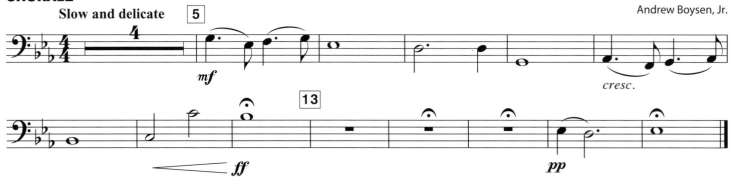

CHORALE

Andante

Robert Sheldon

22

Concert C Minor

150   **PASSING THE TONIC**

151   **BREATHING AND LONG TONES**

152   **CONCERT C NATURAL MINOR SCALE**

153   **CONCERT C HARMONIC AND MELODIC MINOR SCALES**

154   **SCALE PATTERN**

155   **CONCERT C CHROMATIC SCALE**

156   **FLEXIBILITY**

157   **FLEXIBILITY**

8 ARPEGGIOS

9 ARPEGGIOS

0 INTERVALS

1 INTERVALS

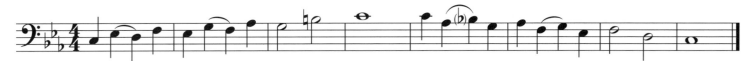

2 BALANCE AND INTONATION: DIATONIC HARMONY

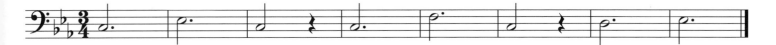

3 BALANCE AND INTONATION: MOVING CHORD TONES

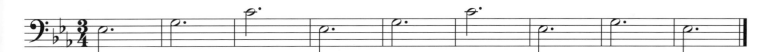

4 BALANCE AND INTONATION: LAYERED TUNING

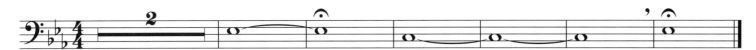

5 BALANCE AND INTONATION: FAMILY BALANCE

6 EXPANDING INTERVALS: DOWNWARD IN TRIADS

7 EXPANDING INTERVALS: UPWARD IN TRIADS

168 RHYTHM

169 RHYTHM

170 RHYTHM

171 RHYTHMIC SUBDIVISION

172 RHYTHMIC SUBDIVISION

173 ARTICULATION AND DYNAMICS

174 ETUDE

Concert F Major

180 **PASSING THE TONIC**

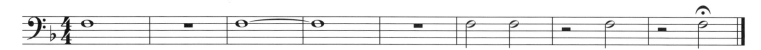

181 **BREATHING AND LONG TONES**

182 **CONCERT F MAJOR SCALE**

183 **SCALE PATTERN**

184 **SCALE PATTERN**

185 **CONCERT F CHROMATIC SCALE**

186 **FLEXIBILITY**

187 **FLEXIBILITY**

ARPEGGIOS

ARPEGGIOS

INTERVALS

BALANCE AND INTONATION: DIATONIC HARMONY

BALANCE AND INTONATION: FAMILY BALANCE

BALANCE AND INTONATION: LAYERED TUNING

BALANCE AND INTONATION: MOVING CHORD TONES

BALANCE AND INTONATION: SHIFTING CHORD QUALITIES

EXPANDING INTERVALS: DOWNWARD IN PARALLEL FIFTHS

EXPANDING INTERVALS: UPWARD IN PARALLEL FIFTHS

28

198 RHYTHM

199 RHYTHM

200 RHYTHM

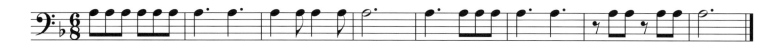

201 RHYTHMIC SUBDIVISION

202 RHYTHMIC SUBDIVISION

203 ARTICULATION AND DYNAMICS

204 ETUDE

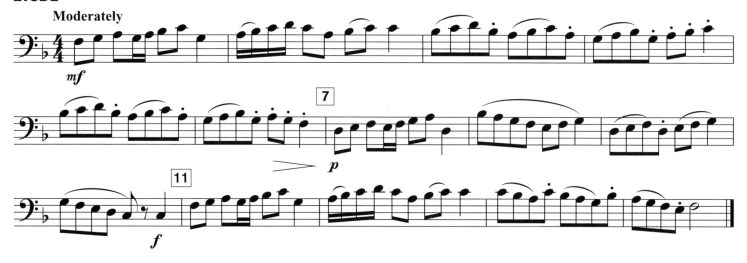

Concert D Minor

210 PASSING THE TONIC

211 BREATHING AND LONG TONES

212 CONCERT D NATURAL MINOR SCALE

213 CONCERT D HARMONIC AND MELODIC MINOR SCALES

214 SCALE PATTERN

215 SCALE PATTERN

216 CONCERT D CHROMATIC SCALE

217 FLEXIBILITY

FLEXIBILITY

ARPEGGIOS

ARPEGGIOS

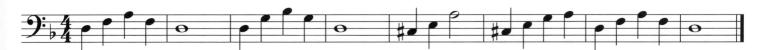

INTERVALS

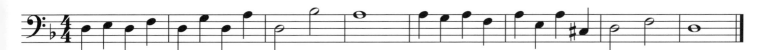

BALANCE AND INTONATION: DIATONIC HARMONY

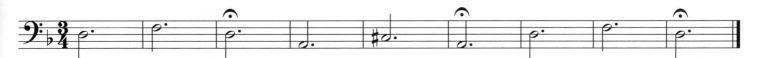

BALANCE AND INTONATION: FAMILY BALANCE

BALANCE AND INTONATION: LAYERED TUNING

BALANCE AND INTONATON: MOVING CHORD TONES

EXPANDING INTERVALS: DOWNWARD IN TRIADS

EXPANDING INTERVALS: UPWARD IN TRIADS

228 **RHYTHM**

229 **RHYTHM**

230 **RHYTHM**

231 **RHYTHMIC SUBDIVISION**

232 **RHYTHMIC SUBDIVISION**

233 **ARTICULATION AND DYNAMICS**

234 **ETUDE**

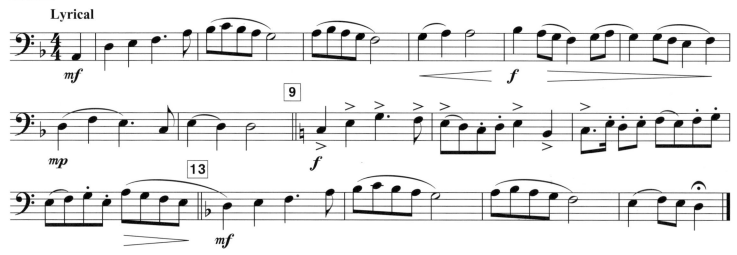

CHORALE

Roland Barrett

CHORALE

Slow and grave

Andrew Boysen, Jr.

CONCERT D MINOR SCALE & CHORALE

Chris M. Bernotas (ASCAP)

CHORALE

Andante

Robert Sheldon

CHORALE: PSALM 33

From the Genevan Psalter
Harmonized by Claude Goudimel (c. 1520–1572)
Arranged/Edited by Todd Stalter

Grave

Concert A♭ Major

240 **PASSING THE TONIC**

241 **BREATHING AND LONG TONES**

242 **CONCERT A♭ MAJOR SCALE**

243 **SCALE PATTERN**

244 **SCALE PATTERN**

245 **CONCERT A♭ CHROMATIC SCALE**

246 **FLEXIBILITY**

247 **FLEXIBILITY**

ARPEGGIOS

ARPEGGIOS

INTERVALS

BALANCE AND INTONATION: DIATONIC HARMONY

BALANCE AND INTONATION: FAMILY BALANCE

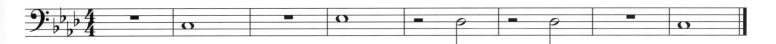

BALANCE AND INTONATION: LAYERED TUNING

BALANCE AND INTONATION: MOVING CHORD TONES

EXPANDING INTERVALS: DOWNWARD IN PARALLEL FIFTHS

EXPANDING INTERVALS: UPWARD IN PARALLEL THIRDS

257 **RHYTHM**

258 **RHYTHM**

259 **RHYTHM**

260 **RHYTHMIC SUBDIVISION**

261 **RHYTHMIC SUBDIVISION**

262 **DYNAMICS**

263 **ARTICULATION AND DYNAMICS**

264 **ETUDE**

Concert F Minor

270 **PASSING THE TONIC**

271 **BREATHING AND LONG TONES**

272 **CONCERT F NATURAL MINOR SCALE**

273 **CONCERT F HARMONIC AND MELODIC MINOR SCALES**

274 **SCALE PATTERN**

275 **CONCERT F CHROMATIC SCALE**

276 **FLEXIBILITY**

277 **FLEXIBILITY**

278 **ARPEGGIOS**

ARPEGGIOS

INTERVALS

INTERVALS

BALANCE AND INTONATION: DIATONIC HARMONY

BALANCE AND INTONATION: FAMILY BALANCE

BALANCE AND INTONATION: LAYERED TUNING

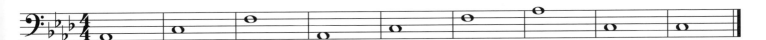

BALANCE AND INTONATION: MOVING CHORD TONES

EXPANDING INTERVALS: DOWNWARD IN TRIADS

EXPANDING INTERVALS: UPWARD IN TRIADS

288 RHYTHM

289 RHYTHM

290 RHYTHM

291 RHYTHMIC SUBDIVISION

292 RHYTHMIC SUBDIVISION

293 ARTICULATION AND DYNAMICS

294 ETUDE

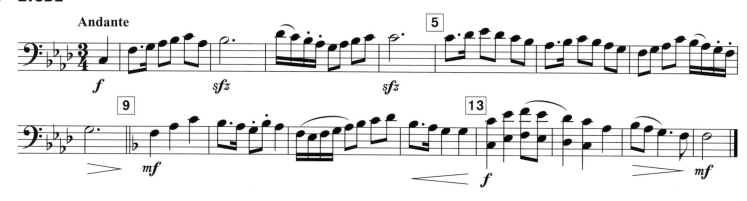

CHORALE

Randall D. Standridge (ASCAP)

Concert D♭ Major

300 **BREATHING AND LONG TONES**

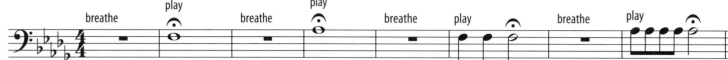

301 **CONCERT D♭ MAJOR SCALE**

302 **SCALE PATTERN**

303 **SCALE PATTERN**

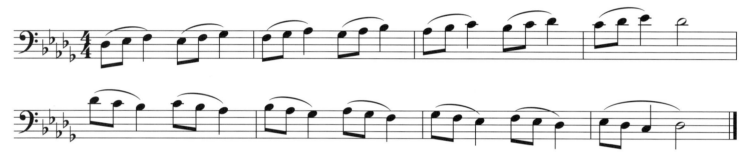

304 **SCALE PATTERN**

305 **FLEXIBILITY**

306 **ARPEGGIOS**

307 **INTERVALS**

BALANCE AND INTONATION: FAMILY BALANCE

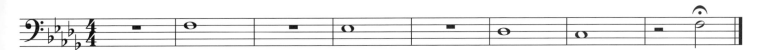

BALANCE AND INTONATION: LAYERED TUNING

EXPANDING INTERVALS: DOWNWARD AND UPWARD IN PARALLEL OCTAVES

ARTICULATION AND DYNAMICS

ETUDE

ETUDE

CHORALE

Andrew Boysen, Jr.

CHORALE

Todd Stalter

Concert B♭ Minor

316 BREATHING AND LONG TONES

317 CONCERT B♭ NATURAL MINOR SCALE

318 CONCERT B♭ HARMONIC AND MELODIC MINOR SCALES

319 SCALE PATTERN

320 SCALE PATTERN

321 FLEXIBILITY

322 ARPEGGIOS

323 INTERVALS

324 BALANCE AND INTONATION: LAYERED TUNING

45

BALANCE AND INTONATION: MOVING CHORD TONES

EXPANDING INTERVALS: DOWNWARD IN TRIADS

ARTICULATION AND DYNAMICS

ETUDE

ETUDE

CHORALE

Michael Story (ASCAP)

CHORALE

Robert Sheldon

Concert C Major

332 **BREATHING AND LONG TONES**

333 **CONCERT C MAJOR SCALE**

334 **SCALE PATTERN**

335 **SCALE PATTERN**

336 **FLEXIBILITY**

337 **ARPEGGIOS**

338 **INTERVALS**

339 **INTERVALS**

340 **BALANCE AND INTONATION: FAMILY BALANCE**

47

BALANCE AND INTONATION: LAYERED TUNING

EXPANDING INTERVALS: DOWNWARD IN PARALLEL FIFTHS

ARTICULATION AND DYNAMICS

ETUDE

Stately

ETUDE

CHORALE

Flowingly
molto legato

Ralph Ford (ASCAP)

9 **A tempo**

CHORALE: LARGO FROM THE "NEW WORLD SYMPHONY"

Antonín Dvořák
Arranged by Michael Story (ASCAP)

Andante
legato

9

48

Concert A Minor

348 BREATHING AND LONG TONES

349 CONCERT A NATURAL MINOR SCALE

350 CONCERT A HARMONIC AND MELODIC MINOR SCALES

351 SCALE PATTERN

352 FLEXIBILITY

353 ARPEGGIOS

354 INTERVALS

355 INTERVALS

356 BALANCE AND INTONATION: DIATONIC HARMONY

BALANCE AND INTONATION: FAMILY BALANCE

EXPANDING INTERVALS: DOWNWARD IN TRIADS

ARTICULATION AND DYNAMICS

ETUDE

Slowly, with feeling

ETUDE

Moderately

CHORALE

Adagio

Todd Stalter

CHORALE

Roland Barrett

Concert G Major

364 **CONCERT G MAJOR SCALE**

365 **BALANCE AND INTONATION: FAMILY BALANCE**

366 **ETUDE**

367 **CHORALE**

Michael Story (ASCAP)

Concert E Minor

368 **CONCERT E NATURAL MINOR SCALE**

369 **CONCERT E HARMONIC AND MELODIC MINOR SCALES**

370 **BALANCE AND INTONATION: LAYERED TUNING**

371 **ETUDE**

372 **CHORALE**

Chris M. Bernotas (ASCAP)

Advancing Rhythm and Meter

$\frac{6}{8}$ METER

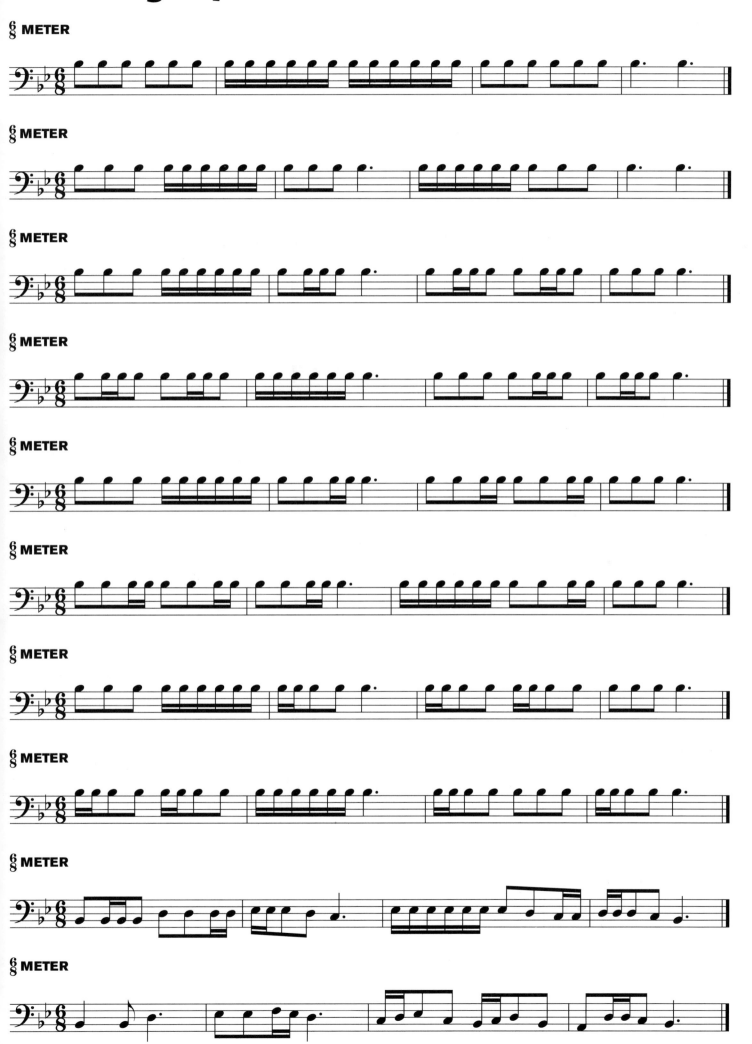

$\frac{6}{8}$ METER

$\frac{6}{8}$ METER

$\frac{6}{8}$ METER

$\frac{6}{8}$ METER

$\frac{6}{8}$ METER

$\frac{6}{8}$ METER

$\frac{6}{8}$ METER

$\frac{6}{8}$ METER

$\frac{6}{8}$ METER

52

383 $\frac{6}{8}$ **METER**

384 $\frac{6}{8}$ **METER**

385 $\frac{6}{8}$ **METER**

386 $\frac{6}{8}$ **METER**

387 $\frac{6}{8}$ **METER**

388 $\frac{6}{8}$ **METER**

389 $\frac{6}{8}$ **METER**

390 $\frac{6}{8}$ **METER**

391 **CHANGING METERS: $\frac{4}{4}$ AND $\frac{6}{8}$**

392 **CHANGING METERS: $\frac{3}{4}$ AND $\frac{6}{8}$**

TRIPLETS

TRIPLETS

TRIPLETS

TRIPLETS

TRIPLETS

TRIPLETS

TRIPLETS

TRIPLETS

TRIPLETS

TRIPLETS

403 **3/8 METER**

404 **3/8 METER**

405 **9/8 METER**

406 **9/8 METER**

407 **12/8 METER**

408 **12/8 METER**

409 **5/8 METER**

(2+3)　　　　　　　　　　　　(3+2)

410 **5/8 METER**

(2+3)　　　　　　　　　　　　(3+2)

411 **7/8 METER**

(2+2+3)

412 **7/8 METER**

(2+2+3)

Trombone Slide Position Chart

This diagram indicates where the top of the slide is located in each position.

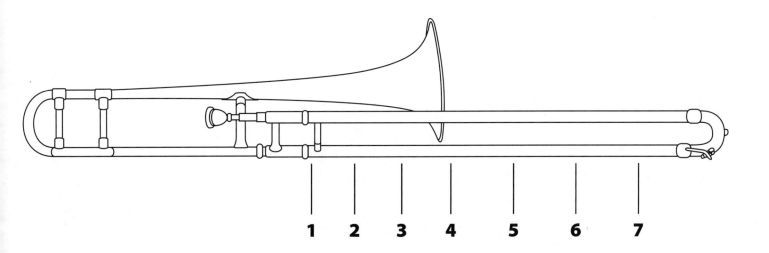

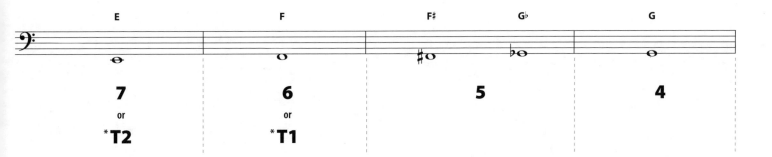

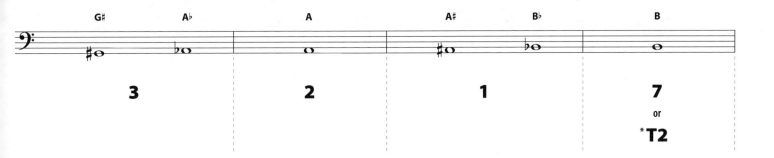

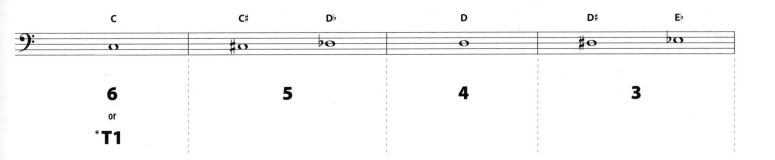

*If playing on an instrument with an F attachment, "T" slide positions should be used.

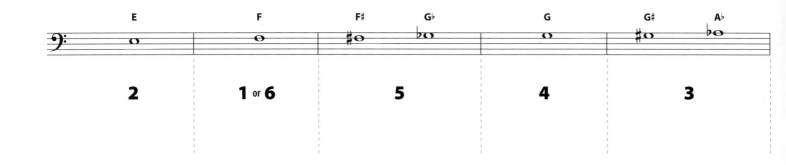

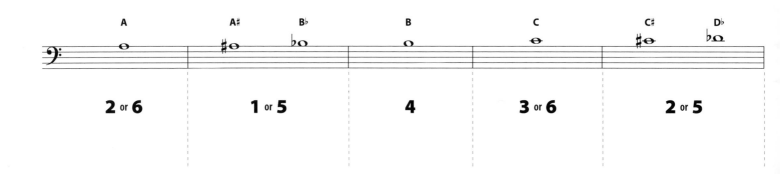

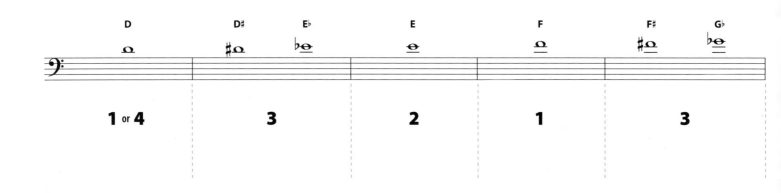